Olde New England's
CURIOUS CUSTOMS AND CURES

This book is dedicated to Richard "Babe" Plante of Salem, Massachusetts, a man of French and Indian stock, noted for his curative powers—he even cured me.

A warrior of the Kickapoo Tribe, from whom we derived "Kickapoo Juice," *a cure-all medicine that saved (and possibly killed) many of our forefathers. Photo courtesy of the Bureau of American Ethnology, Washington.*

© Copyright, Old Saltbox, 1990 ISBN:

Cover Photos: *"Little Whirlwind,"* a painting by noted New York artist Ken Schmidt, is a Mohawk Warrior with a black hand covering his mouth, meaning that he is an elite killer of enemy war chiefs. He was the most feared by other New England Indians, not only for his fighting skills, but because he was known to eat the lungs, heart and liver of his victims.

(Front cover painting by Ken Schmidt, courtesy of Lone Feather Studio, New York.

Engraving of 1750 book by E. Smith, titled "Complete-Housewife—Being a Collection of upwards of Six Hundred Receipts in Cookery, Medicines, Drinks, Syrups, Salves, Ointments, and various other things of Sovereign and approved Efficacy in most Distempers, Pains, Aches, Wounds and Sores."

INTRODUCTION

It seems today that everyone has a cure for every ailment, and all are willing and anxious to reveal their remedies to you especially when you or a loved one is ill. On television and radio, we are constantly bombarded with *"take this for that and that for this,"* yet nobody has discovered how to eliminate the common cold. As for preventatives, Americans seem especially obsessed about things to do and not to do, eat and not eat in order to avoid certain diseases.

In the olden days, believe it or not, things were worse—everyone had a remedy or a preventative, and most were wrong. Doctors usually weren't educated or trained, and many were known as quacks who invented cures with mysterious ingredients or suggested food and drink that might intensify the illness. Seeking help from a healing witch or Indian medicine man could be dangerous, and possibly all they'd do is mumble a few words of magic or perform some sadistic ritual in an attempt to make the sufferer well again. Some Indian remedies, however, discovered before the White man came to these shores, worked well and are still being used to this day. As Smithsonian Institute ethnologist Frances Densmore, explains it in her book, *"How Indians Use Wild Plants for Food, Medicine & Crafts,"* various herb-weeds growing in the forests and wetlands *"were used in the treatment of the sick and in the working of charms."* And she adds that, *"songs were sung to make the treatment and the charms effective."*

Our first New England settlers were plagued with almost every sickness and disease imaginable, the extreme heat and cold and the soggy wetlands where they chose to dwell razed havoc with them. The female homesteader was chief cook and bottle-washer and usually the only doctor-nurse available. Her home remedies were based on Indian cure-alls or old world traditions, many of them steeped in superstition and ancient customs. Like the Indians, they often concluded it was evil powers that caused all sicknesses, and only some diabolical ritual would keep the infectious devil from their door. It was a wild brutal land they lived in, where devastating plagues wiped out half of the first settlers and more than half of the Indians—for those remaining, sickness often racked their bodies and unfounded fears taunted their minds.

Bob Cahill

The all powerful Powahee or Medicine-man of the early 1600's, portrayed here as "Sudden Thunder," by artist Ken Schmidt. Most of New England's early settlers acknowledged the miracles of the Powahees, but believed that their powers came from the devil.

Portrait, courtesy of Lone Feather Studio, New York.

I
Indian Rituals And Remedies

New England's so-called *"savages"* lived in a spiritual world with *"The Great Spirit"* as their protector. Their belief in this heavenly power was great, if not greater than that of their antagonists, the *"holier than thou,"* Pilgrims and Puritans. Indians not only believed they were filled with an inner spirit that communicated with this power, but that all animals, birds, trees and plants did so as well. These Native Americans were instilled with a love and respect for the land and all living creatures. For the most part, they practiced what they preached, whereas America's first White settlers often fell short of this commendable virtue.

In a sermon at Plymouth in 1620, Reverend Cushman said, *"The Indians are thought to be the most cruel and treacherous people in all these parts, even like lions, but to us they have been like lambs, so submissive and trusting, as a man may truly say, many Christians are not so kind and sincere."* A few years later, Roger Williams, founder of Rhode Island, and the first to learn the Indians' language, said that, *"they are wise in natural things beyond the White Man, and are so modest that they shame our English."*

"All is diabolical among the Indians," Cotton Mather, the leading religious spokesman for the Puritans, wrote to London friends from Boston in the mid 1600's, *"our Missionaries have little luck."* In his book, *"Memorable Providences,"* Mather writes, *"the Indians worship the devil, and in their Powwows, often raise their masters in the shapes of bears and snakes and fires."* Actually, the Indians had never heard of the devil until the first White settlers arrived in New England. Their evil spirits were *"Hobbamocho,"* who caused mischief and fear among them, and *"Mahtahdo,"* who was the creator of fights, fevers and flies. The Indians did worship these evil spirits as gods, often offering sacrifices to them, as Reverend Henry White of Boston said, *"to keep them in good humor."*

In 1616, two years after English explorer John Smith and his crew first mapped the New England coast, *Mahtahdo* attacked the Indians with a devastating fever and plague from which they never really recovered. An estimated 80% of New England's coastal Indians were wiped out. *"They died in heaps,"* wrote Thomas Morton, who was arrested a few years later for selling whiskey and firearms to the remaining Indians. *"It seems as if God hath provided this New England country for our nation,"* wrote John Smith, *"destroying the natives by the plague."*

It was Smith who named the Indian village of Patuxet, "Plymouth," and this was where his Captain Thomas Hunt captured twenty Indians in 1615 and brought them to Europe for display. The Pilgrims found the place deserted in 1620 when they came to settle in the New World, for the entire Patuxet Indian population had been wiped out by the plague. The only

Patuxet survivors were those that Captain Hunt had kidnapped. The first Indian to greet the Pilgrims at Plymouth came four months after they arrived, and half their number had died from sickness and exposure to the cold. He was *"Somoset,"* from Monhegan Island, Maine, one of the captives who had spent years in Europe and then returned to New England. If it wasn't for this wandering Sagamore from Maine, the Pilgrims wouldn't have lasted more than a few more months in America. Somoset not only introduced them to their friendly Indian neighbors, but was instrumental in teaching them how to live off the land.

The *"Powahees,"* or *"Shamans,"* as Indian witch-doctors were called, met in a nearby swamp for three days soon after the Pilgrims arrived, deciding how to rid the area of this new White menace. They disagreed with each other on what course of action to take, and while they debated, Somoset went to *Sachem Massasoit* of the Wampanoag nation in what is now Rhode Island, to tell him that the Pilgrims came in peace. This chief of *"the people of the first light,"* which is the meaning for the name *"Wampanoag,"* then visited and befriended the Pilgrims, but the Powahees of Rhode Island's Narragansett nation, convinced their chief to opt for war with the Whites. The Narragansett Indians sent the Pilgrims *"a bundle of arrows tied about with a great snakeskin,"* which was their declaration of war. The Pilgrims returned the package with its Indian messenger to Rhode Island, informing the Narragansett chief that they didn't want war; but musketballs and gunpowder were added to his package, indicating that they weren't afraid to fight either, and that the Whites' weapons were more powerful than his. Many years passed before the Narragansetts caused the Pilgrims any real trouble. Some historians have concluded that the hesitation of these war-like Indians was due to their fear of taking on the Whites in addition to the warriors of the Wampanoag nation. The Narragansetts and Wampanoags had been long standing enemies, and it was some 55 years before they made amends and joined forces to fight the White men, but by then, the military might of the Pilgrims and Puritans was too much for the Indians.

The greatest of New England's Powahees had warned all the Indian nations of destruction if they *"made mischief with the White man. You will be rooted off the earth if you do,"* he warned in 1665, ten years before King Philip's War, when his prophecy came true. *Passaconnaway,* chief and medicine-man of the Penacooks of New Hampshire, was almost 100 years old when he gathered the tribes of the plains north of what is now Concord to make his farewell speech and turn his feathered headress over to his son Wonnalancet. Thousands came to listen to him, including White missionary John Elliot, who was awed at the old chief's seemingly supernatural powers. *"He can make fire in snow, conjure up storms and cuddle venomous snakes,"*

Elliot wrote. When a strange comet appeared in the sky over New England in 1616, Passaconnaway predicted that it forewarned a terrible sickness, and the devastating plague on the Indians followed within a few months.

"I am an old oak that has lasted the storms of many winters," he told those gathered at Amoskeag to hear his final words as chief of the Penacooks. *"My eyes are dim and my limbs tremble. The scalplocks that dried before my wigwam told the stories of my victories over the Mohawks who invaded our hunting grounds. Then, in their place, came the Palefaces. The lands of our forefathers were taken from us... I tried the magic of my sorcery in vain. I, who can take in my palm as I would a worm, the rattlesnake. I, who have seen the Great Spirit in dreams, and talked with him awake; I, as brave as the bravest, as strong as the stongest, as wise as the wisest. I am like a reed before their tempest. Now, my children, heed my dying words. The oak will soon break before the whirlwind...I commune with the Great Spirit. He whispers to me, 'Tell your people, peace. Peace is your only hope... Your forests shall fall before their mighty hatchets. At your fishing places, they shall build their houses!'...We must bend before the storm...Peace, peace with the White man is the command of the Great Spirit, and the last wish of Passaconnaway."*

Powahees were doctors, lawyers, holymen, and in the case of Passaconnaway, Indian chief as well, all rolled into one all-powerful man. They would often call for powwows, gathering the tribes together to give speeches or perform rituals for various reasons: to spiritually assist in planting crops, hunting and pottery making, stimulating warriors before battle, releasing evil spirits from sick tribesmen, and cursing enemies or helping friends in trouble. At these gatherings, the Powahee sometimes made a lot of noise; shouting, screeching, singing, mumbling, beating drums, and usually dancing himself into a frenzy to either manifest or frighten off evil spirits. Indians believed that the Powahee healed others while he danced, and that the guardian spirits of dead ancestors took control of his mind and body, speaking to the tribe through him. As other members of the tribe joined him in song and dance, often for hours at a time, these guardian spirits also filled them with a sense of rebirth and reawakening. As White witnesses to these powwows testified, they seemed to provide the Indians with a new energy and courage. When John Smith was captured by New England Indians, he witnessed a powwow directed by a supposedly powerful Powahee. He said that, *"this appeared to me the most like witchcraft of anything...It is either trickery or mistaken notions, whereby they deceived themselves."*

Like witches, Powahees provided themselves and others of the tribe with objects that would ward off evil, and they often delivered evil fetishes to their enemies, like the bundle of arrows tied about with a great snakeskin, which the Narragansetts presented to the Pilgrims. Animal teeth, claws, and horns made into bracelets and necklaces, or worn on the belt, were considered talismans of luck, providing the wearer with the same skills and courage of the animal from which it came. Shells and bones often contained good spirits, but with a certain remark or ritual from the Powahee, bad spirits could enter them - much like the spells and chants of witches that were also thought to manifest evil spirits. Powahees were known to create fetish bundles of various cursed objects which they would secretly attempt to place as close to their enemies as possible—much like the puppets that witches stuck pins into to hurt their enemies. Powahees also had great knowledge of wild herbs and plants that could poison or remedy, and as they successfully used these potions, their magical power increased in the eyes of the beholders. Powahees like Passaconnaway could accurately predict the future, but Smith for one, did not believe that they had psychic abilities. He writes that, *"Before the battle, witch doctors spy on the enemy's motions carefully, and when they find that they have the greatest prospect of success, the old men pretend to conjure or tell what the outcome will be. They do this in a figurative manner which comes to pass nearly as they foretold. Therefore, the young warriors generally believed these old conjurors, which had the tendency to excite them to push on with vigor."*

Passaconnaway, who was considered the most remarkable medicineman and prophet of the New England Indians, told his people, *"the snake can read your heart,"* and that to dream of a snake meant *"an enemy is about to kill you."* The only way to prevent your enemy from succeeding was to kill a snake the next day before noon. Pilgrims and Puritans considered the snake as evil, the devil incarnate, but Indians believed they were brothers of the snake. Rattlesnakes were prevalent in New England and there were many deaths of early settlers from rattlesnake bites, but most Indians believed that rattlesnakes wouldn't bite them. Black snakes and rattlers could charm Indians, however, as they could hypnotize animals and birds, so many Indians were wary of them.

They also had a fear of swallowing a baby snake when drinking from a stream. The snake, they thought, would grow bigger in the stomach eating the food the victim ate each day. The remedy for this crisis was to fast for several days, but to keep smelling food during the fast, eventually drawing the snake out of the mouth. That the snake, and especially the rattlesnake, was thought to have supernatural powers, to be feared but also adored, was further evidenced by Alex Henry, a White captive who was kidnapped by the Indians when he was a child and lived most of his life with them. He wrote that one day, after he had reached adulthood, *"I awoke to discover a rattlesnake two feet from my naked legs. The reptile was coiled, its head raised considerable above its body. I hastened to the canoe to procure my gun, but the Indians begged me to desist. They followed me to the spot with their pipes and tobacco pouches in their hands. I found the snake still coiled. The Indians surrounded it. All addressed it by turns, calling it their 'Grandfather,' but keeping some distance. They filled their pipes and each blew the smoke toward the snake, who appeared to receive it with pleasure. After remaining coiled and receiveing incense for half an hour, it stretched itself along the ground in visible good humor. At last it moved slowly away. The Indians followed it, beseeching it to take care of their families.*

Henry further relates, *" Early next morning, as we proceeded in our canoes, the wind increased and the Indians, alarmed, frequently called on the rattlesnake to come to their assistance. The waves grew high and it blew a hurricane; we expected every moment to be swallowed up. One of the chiefs took a dog, and tying its forelegs, threw it overboard, calling on the snake to preserve us and satisfy its hunger with the dog. But the wind still increased. Another chief scacrificed another dog, with some tobacco, beseeching the snake not to avenge upon the Indians the insult he had received from myself. He assured the snake I was absolutely an Englishman, and a kin neither to him nor the other Indians. One of them observed that if we drowned, it would be for my fault alone, and I ought myself be sacrificed to appease the angry Manito; nor was I without fear that if the situation became worse this would be my fate. Happily for me, the storm at length abated."*

The venom of rattlesnakes was extracted from its root-bladder by the Indians and used to maim and kill their enemies. Arrowpoints and spearheads were dipped into the collected poison by warriors just before battle, and sharp-ended reeds were also splashed with the venom and planted in the ground to hopefully be stepped on by any approaching barefooted enemy. When Rogers' Rangers retreated into Vermont and New Hampshire after their successful raid on an Indian village in Canada in 1759, nine of the Rangers were led into Crawford Notch by an Indian runner. According to Ethan Allen Crawford, the Indian brought the men through this hidden pass in the White Mountains, *"and left these forlorn mortals at the foot of the mountains, after poisoning the leader of the group with a scratch from a rattlesnake's fang. The pain pressed madness into his brain and he flung himself from a high rock and was dashed to pieces."* Alex Henry informs us that snake blood was also used extensively by the Indians, not as a poison but as a cure. Indian squaws were noted for having few difficulties during childbirth, but few Whites realized that the reason was that many squaws drank snake blood just before delivery. *"Wawatam found a snake and secured relief for his daughter-in-law,"* writes Henry. *"It was a small garter-snake. He held it fast as it coiled around his arm, then he cut off its head, catching the blood in a cup. He carried home the blood, mixed it with water and administered two spoonfuls. Within an hour the patient was delivered of a fine child. The remedy never failed.* "

English explorer Martin Pringe who visited the New England coast in 1603 and anchored near Patuxet, encountered tall, handsome Indians in great numbers who *"wore snake-skins six-foot long, which they used for girdles."* He also noticed that they all carried *"bags of tobacco fastened to these girdles."* and he saw, *"many gardens of tobacco."* The year before, Bartholomew Gosnold and his 32 crewmen lived at Cuttyhunk Island off the coast of Massachusetts for over three months, and he reported that some of the Indians he visited *"smoked pipes steeled with copper."* Early Maine explorers also witnessed Indians smoking pipes carved of stone and others made from lobster claws. Roger Williams, one of the first Whites to live with the Indians, wrote, *"Some New England Indians do not smoke, but they are rare birds, generally all the men have a tobacco-bag with a pipe in it. Sometimes they make such great pipes both of wood and stone, that they are two feet long, with men and beasts carved into the bowls. Besides tobacco, the natives used 'Kinnikinnick,' a mixture of tobacco and bark."* They often used the dried aromatic bark of the sassafras tree, or mixed their tobacco with sumac leaves. Sumac and sassafras were two of the main reasons why Pringe and Gosnold came to New England, for both were in demand as medicines in Europe at the time. The clear oil of safrole is still used in medicines, but in the 1600's, sassafras was a cure for scurvy. Even Columbus witnessed Indians smoking *"sukars"* in America in 1492, and when it was revealed that the Indians *"drank"* the smoke of cigars as a cure-all, they became the rage of Europe. First cured of a headache was Queen Catherine de Medici, who was introduced to smoking by the French consul to Portugal, Jean Nicot, from whom we get the word *"nicotine."*

Smoking to the New England Indians wasn't just a pleasurable pastime or habit as it was for the White man—to them, smoking was a sacred ritual. They would fast for days and then smoke for hours to see visions which directed their future actions. The smoke was considered supernatural—a way of communicating with the gods or with long dead ancestors. Unsmoked tobacco was also constantly offered to the gods as a gift or a bribe. The Great Spirit, according to the Indians, loved smoke and was always present when the peacepipe was lit. Tobacco was as precious to the Indians as gold was to the White man. Besides being an element of their worship, when wet with spittle, it could heal infected wounds, and when smoked, it was a panacea for various sicknesses. Although the health of New England Indians was generally good, except for the fatal plagues of small-pox and yellow fever that came with the White man, their only complaint seemed to be periodic lung ailments, due to living in wet weather, and of course, due to smoking. They considered the cure to be either more smoking, or a one hour stint in a hot-house, then a swim in a cold stream or river. Almost all Indian families built hot-houses or used caves as steam baths to "sweat out" illnesses, but smoking was the native aspirin of the 17th century and, apparently, had been for many centuries prior to the White man coming to these shores. The first settlers also grew tobacco for their own pleasure and for export to Europe. It soon became one of America's most valuable commodities, although King James I said that smoking was *"A vile and stinking custom, loathsome to the eye, hateful to the nose, harmful to the brains, and dangerous to the lungs."* We have only just come to realize that the king was right.

Instead of burning tobacco, the Powahee or Shaman would burn sweet-grass and blow the smoke into the nostrils of a sick Indian to rid him of evil spirits. Usually the Shaman wore braided sweet-grass as a mantle or necklace, so as to always have it with him to aide a sick fellow tribesman. Burned sweet-grass could always dispel illnesses inflicted by the evil *Hobbamocho,* but if the usually kind god *"Kiehtan"* was angry at the victim, then nothing the Powahee did could save him from death. Powahees have been known to attempt to release evil or pain from a fellow Indian by using hollow sticks or bones inserted into the ear, mouth, or nose, then blow smoke through them, or suck on them like a straw. They also tried to release demons by cutting holes in the victim's head. Sometimes these unorthodox methods of doctoring worked, probably due to mind over matter, and the techniques would be passed on from one Shaman to another, usually to his son, for the offspring of an Indian medicine-man often became one himself. Daughters of Powahees sometimes became herb doctors, learning secret magical remedies from their fathers, and throughout their lives carrying an otterskin medicine bag tied to their waist, filled with cures. Although most remedies and healing rituals were passed down from one Shaman to another through the ages, many Indians learned the cures to various sicknesses by watching what the wild animals ate when they were ill. Although all the twenty or more Indian nations that inhabited New England had similar customs, ceremonies, and cures, they gave healing plants different names. Also, Shamans often didn't name plants or trees, but would merely point them out to an apprentice and make him learn what sicknesses they cured, and what part: the root, stem, leaf, flower, bark, or berry, held the magic ingredient for healing. There were a few common cures known by all New England Indians that were passed on to the White settlers, and as 18th century historian Samuel Adams Drake wrote, *"The wonderful cures of Indian magicians or medicine-men were thoroughly believed in by the settlers in New England, and are vouched for by White evidence."*

The wet, swampy soil surrounding Plymouth, Salem, and Boston where Whites first settled was the source of many illnesses, including the seemingly ever present fevers and colds. It was the Indian Shaman called Joe Pyeweed by the Pilgrims, who pointed out to them that the cure for flu and fever was a purple flower that grows wild in the meadows of Plymouth. It was then called Queen-of-the-meadow, but it's now called *"Joe Pyeweed,"* so it's obvious that Joe's cure worked for the Whites. Another wild plant called meadowsweet or *"spirea,"* was also used by the Indians and the first White settlers for relieving fevers and headaches, and today we know that spirea contains salicin, and salicin is aspirin. Salicin is also a natural substance found in the bark, leaves, and roots of poplars and willowtrees. New England Indians chewed willow-bark when they had toothaches. By watching crippled wild animals, the Indians learned to chew bullthistles for the pain and stiffness of rheumatism and for anemia, and they also chewed on cowparsnip leaves to find temporary relief for sore and tired limbs. Water-lilies were eaten for indigestion, and ground up mussels were their cure for constipation. For internal ills such as diarrhea or dysentery, which sometimes ravaged the Indians and the first settlers, dried and powdered blackberry leaves mixed with water was one of the best cures. For heat rash and other skin irritations, the Indians saw animals rub their diseased hides on yarrowleaves, so they did the same, and the Whites learned from the Indians, making an ointment from the juice of the leaves. Another skin ointment commonly used by the Indians was the sweet oil from white acorns, and they also used it as a sauce in their meat stews. Raw clams, which were part of the daily diet of the seaside Indians, were also considered a cure-all for internal and external sores and tumors.

Except for a few Maine and Connecticut tribes, New England Indians cultivated herbs, corn, and other vegetables, usually within an acre of land that was set aside for each family near their wigwams, and this was their custom long before the White man came. It was a Patuxet Indian named *"Tisquantum,"* one who Captain Hunt had kidnapped in 1615 and brought to England, who returned to his village in March of 1621 to find the half-starved Pilgrims living there, and taught them how to properly plant their gardens. Indian maize, or corn as we now call it, would not grow ears unless fertilized with dead fish, he informed them, and among other things, he taught them how to fish for eels, which soon became a staple to their meager diet. They learned that the tart but tasty cranberries were not only good to eat and cured scurvy, but that a tea sedative could be made from the bark of the highbush cranberry shrub. Popcorn was introduced, to the delight of the Pilgrim children, and the methods of boiling ginseng-root for food and to enhance fertility, to the delight of the Pilgrim men. Indian Turnip root was not only a fine vegetable, but was also good for staying coughs and rheumatic symptoms, as were pokeweed berries, which could also be used to make a fine wine—and the well-boiled root of the pokeweed was also a vegetable. A strong coffee was made by crushing and roasting the bitter berries of the juniper, and its root was eaten to ease kidney problems, as were the leaves of the wintergreen, which also made a delicious tea. Indian Joe Pyeweed's contribution to cure headaches and fever, also made a wonderful and stimulating drink, so the Pilgrims soon discovered, which they called *"Boneset Tea."*

The first White settlers soon realized that the Indians commonly ate the roots of plants and shrubs growing wild in the marshes, meadows and woods as vegetables in their daily diets, and that some of these roots were remedies for various illnesses. There was one problem, however, and that was that some of these roots were extremely poisonous, which the Indians had learned over the centuries, obviously by trial and error. The smelly Skunk-Cabbage, for example, was boiled and eaten by New England Indians as a cure for bronchitis and whooping cough, yet its root is highly poisonous. Black snakeroot, or *"Cohosh,"* as the Indians called it, was swallowed by those suffering from respiratory problems, but *"Senega,"* also known as Snakeroot, is a poison. Squaw root, taken internally by Indian women to solve various female problems and irritations, if swallowed in large doses could be a killer. Indians dug up the Cocklebur root and made a potion of it to ease pleurisy and stomach pains. They also considered it a blood and skin purifier, but in heavy doses, it too is dangerous. The Penobscots of Maine, after pulverising and boiling the roots of the Pipsissewa weed, drank the water from it as a tonic to induce sweating, which they felt would drive sickness and evil spirits from their bodies, yet they knew that the root was poisonous. They also applied the root externally to swollen limbs and blistered hands and feet. Goldthread, which the Indians called *"Yellow Plant,"*grows in marshes and bogs and is also poisonous, but they applied it to cankers and irritated gums, and made a tonic of it which was swallowed to soothe sore throats. Another common plant of the marshlands that we call *"Cattails"* was consumed by the Indians, the raw shoots and roots either eaten raw or boiled as a vegetable, and their fluffy heads were swallowed as a stopper for diarrhea. The first settlers were soon to realize, as the Indians had discovered long before, *"The cure to an illness can usually be found near its source."*

Well into the 19th century, the few Indians that remained in New England peddled medicines, tonics, and curative salves door-to-door, village to village. Their concoctions were a mystery, the ingredients known only to them. *"My father purchased each Spring from every tall and old Indian who*

Alicia Larson of the Early Sites Research Society, clears away brambles and brush from a sacred Indian Manitou, or what White settlers called a "sacrifice rock." *This Manitou, once an idol of worship for Indians, is located at the Gungywamp archaeological site at Groton, Connecticut. The Manitous of many tribes are located throughout New England; the Mohican stone, where the great Chief Uncas once worshiped, is located in Madison, Connecticut, and the Manitous of the Wampanoags can be found on County Road between Plymouth and Cape Cod.*

Indian Powahee performs the Ghost Dance at a Powwow.
Photos courtesy Early Sites Research Society, Rowley, Massachusetts.

Statue of Wampanoag Chief Massasoit at Plymouth, and photo of Chief ScabbyBull taken in the mid 1800's, showing a remarkable resemblance to the old savior of the Pilgrims. Both carry pipes, the Indian's most cherished possession. Smoking was not only a pleasure and a spiritual experience for the Indians, but the smoke was a cure-all for many ills. Most New England Indians, and especially the chiefs, were buried with their favorite pipe.

Mike Ranco, a Penobscot Indian and descendant of tribal Powahees, is owner of the Turquoise Turtle Indian Store at Belfast, Maine. Recently pestered with ghosts at his home, Mike burned sweetgrass in a basket and circled the house, an ancient Indian remedy for expelling evil spirits. "And it worked," said Mike. Powahees often blew the smoke of burning sweetgrass into the nose, eyes and ears of sick tribe members as a panacea for various ailments.

claimed to be a Penobscot Chief, a bottle labeled 'Kickapoo Indian Sag-waw', " wrote Alice Morse Earle in 1902. "This concoction, which was black and syrupy, emitted a really delectable smell," she added. The common name for all these cure-all tonics was usually "Kickapoo Juice" or "Snake Oil." Many Indians claimed that Snakeroot was the main ingredient of their potions, which they believed contained mystical powers. Echinacea, also called "Indian Head," was often one of the ingredients in Snake Oil, which was effective in healing insect bites. But their tonics could contain anything and everything from over one thousand plants and herbs that their ancestors had discovered and used as healers, all growing wild in the marshlands, forests, and mountains of New England.

One popular Indian cure-all tonic was introduced to Europeans by famous philosopher George Berkeley in the early 18th century. With this miraculous liquid, which Berkeley called "tar-water," he saved an estimated 10,000 lives in Ireland of those who suffered from severe dysentery. Berkeley had learned of this remedy from the Narragansett Indians when he lived in Newport, Rhode Island. Pine-tar had been chewed and swallowed by New England Indians for centuries as a soothing stomach remedy. The pine trees of Maine also provided a similar cure-all for stomach trouble, and was first noted by explorer George Waymouth in 1605. "There are Fir Trees here," he wrote, "out of which issueth Turpentine in so marvellous plenty and so sweet, never seen as good in England." Penobscot Indians to this day, scrape the gum off the bark of the Balsam Fir to cover and heal cuts and burns, and during battles, Maine Indians used the gummy substance to clean wounds. Although we wouldn't think of swallowing turpentine as a medicine today, the first White settlers found it most efficient for "settling the bowels."

Captive Alex Henry, after many years of living with the Indians, reported that "the Indians are in general, free from disorders, but the remedies they most rely on are emetics, cathartics and the lancet, especially the last." The lancet was a small two-edged surgical knife always carried and constantly used by doctors in Colonial Days to bleed patients, a remedy for purifying the blood. Alex Henry concluded that bleeding was the most popular remedy among Indians as well. "Whether sick or well," Henry writes, "I have sometimes seen a dozen women in the morning as they sat in a row along a fallen tree, bleeding each other with sharp lancets." Since the knife was unknown to American Indians until the White man came, one wonders if this was an ancient custom of theirs, possibly using a sharp bone or stone as a cutting implement—or was it something they learned from the Whiteman? Indians were fascinated with knives, to the point that they called New England's first explorers "Knife Men." When the ARCHANGEL arrived at Pemaquid, Maine in May of 1605, George Waymouth took advantage of their obsession by making them think that knives and swords contained supernatural powers. *"He caused his own and Rosier's swords to be touched with the loadstone,"* reported one of the crewmen, which made their swords magnets. *"Then with the blades, took up knives and needles, much mystifying the simple savages with his jugglery."* And so, the first impression of these Maine Indians was that the Whites were gods and their weapons were magical. Their next impression was that the Whites were evil, for after feigning friendship, Waymouth and his men attempted to capture as many of the Indians as possible, and succeeded in bringing a few back in chains to England.

The first New England explorers and the vast majority of settlers considered the ceremonies and rituals of the Indians quite childish and foolish. One ARCHANGEL crewman, Own Griffen, when he first approached a group of Maine Indians on the beach, thought their antics were ridiculous. *"The oldest among them rose up and suddenly cried out with a loud voice, shouting 'Baugh Waugh.' The women fell down and the men stomped the ground about the fire as hard as they could,"* he reported. *"Many took fire sticks and thrust them into the earth. Then the younger ones did fetch stones and they beat them with their sticks. Then, with the stones, beat the earth with all their strength, and in this manner, they continued about two hours."* Cotton Mather considered all their dancing, shouting, fasting and feasting, *"diabolical,"* yet, there were always logical or religious meanings behind their activities. To those who didn't understand, their rituals were silly, meaningless, and even frightening.

Living among the Indians for so long, Alex Henry was constantly urged to participate in their ceremonies, and by so doing, came to understand many of their age-old customs. *"A little child fell into a kettle of boiling syrup,"* he reported. *"It was instantly snatched out, but with little hope of recovery. So long as it lived, a continual feast was observed. This was made to the Great Spirit and Master of Life, that He might be pleased to save and heal the child. At this feast I was a constant guest and often found difficulty in eating the large quantity of food which on such occasions is put upon each man's dish. The Indians accustom themselves both to eat much and to fast much with facility. Several sacrifices were also offered. Among these were dogs killed and hung upon the tops of poles, with the addition of blankets and other articles. These also were given to the Great Spirit."*

Most rituals and sacrifices were performed and provided for the Great Spirit, who they believed dwelled in all things. Some Indians thought that the good god *"Kiechtan"*, who brought them pleasures, was the Great Spirit but most considered Kiechtan a lesser god, like *"Geesukquand,"* spirit of the sun, and *"Nibah-Nahbeezik,"* the water spirit. All were constantly being offered gifts of blankets, wampum, shells, and animal sacrifices for their favors. It was *"Manibozho"* also called *"Manitou,"* who remade the world after a great flood. He was considered by some nations of New England Indians to be the Great Spirit. An old Wampanoag legend is that *Manitou* sent his son *"Weetucks"* to the seacoast Indians years before the White man came. He showed them how to make fire and plant crops and beseeched all Indians to live in peace with each other. He assured them that after death they would all meet again in the Western sky, and then *Weetucks* disappeared *"into the Western heavens."* Sound familiar?

It was an intense belief of New England Indians that the lesser gods and their deceased ancestors visited them while they slept, often providing them with prophetic messages. Dreams and nightmares profoundly influenced their lives and affected most of their actions. These spiritual visitors most often invaded an Indian's sleep with symbolic revelations, and it was the Shaman's job to reveal the hidden meanings of these symbols to the entire tribe. A cunning Shaman, of course, could translate these dream-symbols to meet his own desires. For example, if the chief dreamed of a flying bird and the Shaman wanted the tribe to break camp and move to a new location, then he would suggest that their ancestors were telling them to move out. In order to have these prophetic dreams, an Indian would periodically walk deep into the woods alone and starve himself for days, hoping to hallucinate and receive a vision that would then dictate all his future activities. It was such a vision that saved the life of Alex Henry after being captured by an Indian raiding party and transported to Canada. *"Chief Wawatam had begun to come often to see me,"* wrote Henry, *"and he showed me strong marks of personal regard. After this had continued for some time, he came on a certain day with his whole family, bringing a large present of skins, sugar and dried meat. Laying there in a heap, he informed me that some years before, he had, according to the custom of his nation, gone off alone in the wilderness and observed a fast. By this he hoped to obtain from the Great Spirit protection through all his days. On this occasion, the Great Spirit had given him a dream in which he adopted an Englishman as his son, brother, and friend. From the moment he first beheld me, he had recognized me as the person the Great Spirit had pointed out to him for a brother. He hoped I would not refuse his present, and said he should forever regard me as one of his family."*

Probably the most superstitious Indians about dreams and nightmares, were the Mohegans of Connecticut and the Mohawks of Vermont. These were also considered the most ferocious of the New England Indians. Nightmares seemed to plague them, and it was their belief that if they turned their mocassin soles up on the ground before sleeping, their nightmares would not come true. If an enemy warrior or a dangerous animal entered their dream-world for three nights in a row, they were convinced that the dream would become reality and that the enemy or animal would surely kill them some-time in the near future. If a Mohegan dreamed of the great *"Uncas,"* their leader in the mid 1600s, he would have good health and any sick family member would soon recover; but to dream of a warrior wearing a war-bonnet, or a boiling pot that overflows, meant that a sick tribesman would soon die. To the Mohawks, dreaming of a black animal, a man with a blackened face, or a flock of black birds, was an omen of death. *"Nearly everyone in the tribe believes that to dream of black animals or objects is an evil omen,"*wrote White captive James Smith. *"A black monster with terrible claws and wide spreading wings appears. This is a sign that death will claim the tribe within a short time."* Alex Henry wrote that, *"Chief Wawatam's sleep was fre-quently disturbed with the noise of evil black birds."*

If any Mohegan or Mohawk tribe member heard the hoot of an owl at night before a journey or battle, that event was postponed, for the wise owl was warning them of impending disaster. The Penacooks of New Hamp-shire felt as strongly about the evening cry of a loon. Its lonely cry was a warning from a long dead tribal ancestor. The Penacooks also believed that a screeching hawk circling their campground, once the sun went down, meant death to one of their tribe members. Most Indians, like the Whites, thought that the howling of a dog at night was a death omen, but the mournful howl of a black dog meant death to the Shaman or Chief of the tribe. Explorer Martin Pringe, anchored near Patuxet in 1603, mentions that he had two Mastiff dogs aboard his ship, *"one being black in colour, whom the Indians were more afraid than of twenty of our men."* Yet, there was hardly an In-dian family that didn't have one or two dogs as pets, often earning their keep by hunting and sometimes by hauling loads from one campground to another. Dogs were usually respected by the Indians because they were thought to have a sixth sense perception, but as Alex Henry often witnessed, they were frequently sacrificed to angry gods, and were sometimes eaten when there was a scarcity of wild animals to hunt.

To the Indians, hunting was the most sacred of daily activities, for to kill an animal was to kill a brother. When the animal was killed, a thank you prayer was offered to the Great Spirit, and upon eating the animal, In-dians believed that the hunter would gain some of its strength, swiftness, cunning, or whatever other qualities that animal might have had in life. The hunter usually received the liver of the animal as his share to eat, for the liver contained all the animal's virtues. Even all the games Indians played had hidden religious significance, which the first White Settlers did not com-prehend. The game of kickball or football, played much like American football is played today but without protective padding, was actually a religious ceremony performed for the Great Spirit so that He might bring them rain for their crops. An animal bladder was usually used for a ball, the goalposts were miles apart, and the game continued on for days. A similar game, called by the Wampanoags, *"fire-ball"* was like soccer, and was played only when a Chief was ill. It was a healing ceremony to please the Great Spirit.

Settled into America only 16 months, word came to the Pilgrims that their new-found friend Massasoit, Chief of the Wampanoags, was dying. All cures, ceremonies and sacrifices had been tried without avail by the Indians. This was a great dilemma for the Pilgrims, for without Massasoit, the Whites had no ally in this savage land. Two Pilgrims were sent to Massassoit's village of Sowans in Rhode Island, carrying with them White man's medicine in an attempt to save him. When they arrived, they found that the great Sachem had lost his eyesight and was choking on his own phlegm. He was fading fast, and with him, the Pilgrims' hope and desire for a lasting peace. A few spoonfuls of the White man's medicine and Massasoit sat up and walked from his wigwam. Immediately his sight and spunkiness returned. *"I will never forget this kindness,"* he told the Pilgrims Winslow and Hampden, *"you have saved my life."* Massasoit was true to his word, and peace with the neighboring Indians lasted for over fifty years, war commencing only a few months after Massasoit died of old age in 1675. The miraculous medicine served up by the Pilgrims and blessed by the Great Spirit to preserve peace, was described only as *"a herb broth."* Could it be that this remarkable remedy was—what is considered today as America's foremost panacea for every sickness imaginable, brought to us from the tribes of Israel—*chicken soup?*

When the Great War with the Indians began, there were some 33,000 Whites living in New England. Wampanoag warriors inspired by *Metacomet,* Massasoit's son, attacked the White village of Swansea on the Massachusetts—Rhode Island border. Six Swansea farmers were killed, and when a makeshift army of 400 men was sent out of Boston to battle Metacomet, who the Whites called *"King Philip,"* they found only the heads of the six farmers mounted on long poles. This ghastly sight was the first indication for many settlers of the brutality of their new enemy. Yet, for the Indian's, the cutting off of a dead man's head or the shaving off of his scalp, was merely a customary battle ritual. The head or scalp-lock was a trophy, an emblem of bravery to be displayed. Usually the severed heads or scalps of enemies were brought back for display in the Indian villages, hung outside warrior wigwams. This was also a ritual of the ancient Celtics, the scalps substituting for the heads when they became too cumbersome to carry all the way back to the village. Erroneously, some historians claimed that only the Mohawks and Mohegans took bloody trophies, and that Indians scalped their victims only because White men were willing to pay for scalps—the French paying for English scalps and the English paying for French scalps. The first record of a head being cut off as a trophy in battle in New England is revealed in the 1606 Journal of Samuel Champlain, when he and his crew encountered hostile Indians at Chatham, Cape Cod. In a battle at Stage Harbor, three Frenchmen and seven Wampanoags were killed. After Champlain invited the Indians to eat with him, he and his men cut off their heads—so, the Whites and not the Indians were the first head-loppers in New England!

Brutal tortures by Indians of captured enemies were common, for the Indians felt it allowed the captive to display courageous endurance, a quality the Indians greatly admired. From early childhood, Indians were taught to withstand great physical pain and never to cry out no matter how intense the pain. The Mohegans, who allied with the Whites in King Philip's War, were most cruel in their treatment of fellow Indian captives, but Metacomet's warriors remakably endured, sometimes singing or taunting the Mohegans as their fingers and hands were being cut off. Indians did not mistreat captive women and children, however, and in fact treated them humanely, usually inviting them to become members of their tribe. Many kidnapped White children, after living with the Indians, preferred their new way of life and balked at returning to the White world when rescued or offered release for ransom. Mary Rowlandson, captured after an attack by Metacomet's braves on Lancaster, Massachusetts, once released, said that, *"I have been in the midst of those roaring lions and savage bears day and night, and sleeping all sorts together, yet not one of them ever offered the least abuse of unchastity to me."*

Charles Johnson, a later captive, related: *"The Indian arrived and brought the heart-chilling news that my fellow prisoner, William Flynn had been burnt at the stake and devoured by the savages at one of the towns. This monster declared that he had been present when the miserable man was sacrificed and had partaken of the horrid banquet. He said that Flynn's flesh was sweeter than any bear's meat, a food in highest repute with the Indians."*

Alex Henry writes that after a battle, his Indian mentor, Chief Wawatam, was called to join other Chiefs *"to take part in a feast. Wawatam obeyed the summons, taking with him his dish and spoon. After about half an hour he returned bringing in his dish a human hand and a large piece of flesh. He did not appear to relish the repast, but told me it always had been the custom among all the Indian nations when returning from war to make a war feast from among the slain. This, he said, inspired the warriors with courage in the attack."* The Mohegans especially, it was reported during King

Philip's War and during the Pequot War of 1637, relished eating the hearts of fallen enemy warriors. *"They all partook,"* writes a Colonial eyewitness, *"sitting in a circle and each taking a bite out of the heart."* The Mohawks too, obviously indulged in cannibalism, for their name in Iroquois language means *"flesh eaters."* Their belief was that by eating the enemy, especially his heart, you gained his courage, strength, wisdom and other positive traits, just like the rewards gained by eating the liver of an animal killed in the hunt. Actually, by eating your slain foe, you honored him. Then, to appease the victim's family, an Indian who killed another in combat, would present the family with gifts and often care for their every need.

If this custom weren't enough to upset the faint-hearted, Alex Henry takes us one step further in revealing horrific rituals of our Native Americans. He found himself one day in the midst of an Indian attack on a White fort: *"I beheld the ferocious triumphs of the barbarian conquerors. The dead were scalped and mangled, the dying were writhing and shrieking under the knife and tomahawk. From the bodies of some, ripped open, these butchers were drinking the blood, scooped up in the hollow of joined hands, and quaffed amid shouts of rage and victory."*Again, as repugnant as this seems, drinking the blood of a slain enemy, so some Indian warriors believed, provided the partaker with the strength and courage of the victim. It is obvious why stories such as these filled New Englanders with justifiable fear. But the brutalities of the Whites in war with the Indians were just as repulsive.

When Chief Metacomet was finally cornered and slain on August 12, 1676, he was chopped into pieces: one of his hands was sent to Boston for display, the other was kept by the Indian who killed him; his feet were delivered to the Whites of Providence, Rhode Island; other parts of his anatomy were shipped to Connecticut; and his head went to Plymouth, where it was exhibited, hung on a pole in the middle of town for twenty-five years. Nine months after Metacomet was unceremoiously dismembered, Cotton Mather mentions in a letter that, *"the women at Marblehead, as they came out of the meeting-house, fell upon two Indians that were brought in as captives, and in a tumultuous way, very barbarously murdered them."* Many of King Philip's warriors were hunted down after the war was over and were killed, others were asked to surrender, and when they did, they were executed. Many Indians who had remained neutral during the war were shipped off to the West Indies, as were Metacomet's wife and son, as slaves. Only a few managed to escape into Canada. The Indians were judged by their actions in war and not for their many kindnesses in peace. Few Indians were left in New England after King Philip's War, and most of them were herded together and made to live in designated reservations. Powahee Passaconnaway's prediction came true: *"Take heed how much you quarrel with the En-*

glish, "he had warned, *"for though you may do them much mischief, you will be destroyed and rooted off the earth if you do."*

Before opting for war with the Whites, King Philip and his Sagamore Annawon, had journeyed to Mount Wachusett to consult with a great Powahee who lived with the Nipmuck Indians. This Powahee kept a large turtle for consulting purposes, the turtle being more sacred than the snake as a messenger from their gods and ancestors. Metacomet asked if he should keep the peace with the Pilgrims and Puritans, or should he, *"drive them back into the sea from where they came."* The Powahee asked the turtle, but it was asleep, its head tucked into its shell, but as Annawon approached it, the head quickly came out from under the shell and it began snapping at Annnawon's arm. King Philip had his answer. A sleeping turtle decided the fate of the New England Indians, and they were *"rooted off the earth"*— their colorful rituals and many of their helpful remedies uprooted with them.

Today's Supreme Powahee of the Wampanoag Indians is "Slow Turtle," *portrayed here in native dress by artist Ken Schmidt.*
Courtesy Lone Feather Studio, New York.

Chief Metacomet, son of Massasoit, better known as "King Phillip," from a 17th century sketch. Because a sacred turtle snapped at his favorite warrior, he waged war on the Whites and caused the expulsion of most Indians from New England to Canada and the West Indies.

Scalping was an Indian ritual and probably had been long before the White man came to these shores. It also had been a ritual of the ancient Celtics. This engraving depicting the barbarity of Indians, appeared first in England in Thomas Anbury's 1789 book, "Travels Through the Interior Parts of America." *The first scalping in New England, however, was by White men on Indians at Cape Cod.*

Old Indian totem poles of sacred animals have disappeared but new ones have recently been sculptured in wood, like the one shown here at Bar Harbor, Maine.

The circle has always been sacred to the Indians. Here at the beginning of the Mohawk Trail in Western Massachusetts, a circular monument representing New England's Indian nations sits beneath the Mohawk Indian statue, "Hail To The Sunrise."

On the rock upon which this life-sized statue stands at the entrance to the Mohawk Trail is a plaque which reads: "HAIL TO THE SUNRISE— MOHAWK INDIAN—The Mohawks of the Five Nations. . . . For 90 Great Suns They Fought the New England Tribes. The New York Mohawks That Traveled This Trail Were Friendly To The White Settlers."

With the New England Indians literally "rooted off the earth," the Puritans searched for and found another scapegoat, the old herb-healers, who they called witches. Most were old women who the Puritans believed could harm as well as heal by giving their victims the "evil eye," or the "evil touch." The few doctors of 17th century New England were untrained, and many were quacks. They envied these old women who produced remedies from their gardens. Doctors had hands of hanging victims cut off, and the severed hands were used by them in an attempt to cure victims of various diseases. Dr. Quincy, for one, believed that "strooking a tumour with a dead hand, will dissolve the tumour."

Photo of dead hand of a witch, courtesy British Museum, London.
Sketch by Trish Cahill, courtesy Witch Dungeon Museum, Salem, MA.

A 16th century engraving of witches concocting a brew that gave them the power to fly on broomsticks, by Hans Green.

Puritan ministers of the 1600's not only struggled to save souls, but to save the bodies of their parishioners as well, by concocting various cure-alls for sicknesses and diseases. Their formulas for remedies were often as foolhardy as the first country doctors, most of whom mixed a variety of foul ingredients to administer to their trusting patients, the patients sometimes dying as a result.

Most of those accused and condemned as witches in the 1600's, were herb-healers who practiced medicine passed on from their European ancestors and from Indian medicine-men. Like the Powahees, these women became too powerful in the eyes of the Puritan ministers. In 1692, many were arrested, jailed, and 19 were hanged at Gallows Hill, Salem.

Photos courtesy the Witch Dungeon Museum, Salem, and Night Owl Productions, Nahant, MA, from the American Playhouse Production mini-series, *"Three Sovereigns For Sarah."*

Colonial Quacks And Kickapoo Juice

Increase and Cotton Mather, father and son, were considered the most learned men in New England in the 17th century. They were Puritan ministers, as were two generations of male Cottons and Mathers before them. Cotton Mather's grandfathers were Reverend Richard Mather and Reverend John Cotton, and all their female offspring: daughters, granddaughters and great-granddaughters, married ministers. They were also upper-middle class aristocrats, who looked down their noses at the poor and despised the rich. As the title *"Puritans"* implies, the Mathers and their followers considered themselves *"pure"* and would allow no impurities among them, such as Quakers, Baptists, Episcopalians, Catholics, or Indians, the latter whom they tolerated only long enough to usurp their land. In Puritan society, only a *"Freeman"*, who owned property worth over 200 pounds, could vote or involve himself in governmental affairs. The Freemen of Boston, Cambridge, Charlestown, Salem, and surrounding towns and villages, made up only 20% of the population of the Massachusetts Bay Colony, and by law, they were to be called *"Mister."* The poorer majority were called *"Goodmen,"* and their wives, *"Goodwife,"* but they had little say in the workings of their government or their religion. Below them were indentured servants, usually boys and girls from the slums of England, Scotland, Ireland, and Wales who worked for some seven to twelve years before they obtained their freedom; and black slaves, brought from Africa via the West Indies, as early as 1634, who seldom found freedom here in New England for over a century. The Pilgrims were more tolerant of outsiders, Indians, and poor people than the Puritans, mainly because the Pilgrims were poor themselves and not as strict in their religious dogmas, nor as greedy in their pursuits to capitalize on their new homeland.

Edward Ward, an English traveler to New England in 1699, wrote of the Puritans: *"they seem very religious, showing many outward and visible signs of an inward and spiritual Grace, but though they wear in their faces the innocence of doves, you will find them in their dealings as subtle as serpents. Interest in their faith, money, their God and large possessions, the only heaven they covet."* Mark Twain said, *"the Puritans first fell upon their knees, and then upon the aborigines."* Cotton Mather continuously called the local Indians *"silly savages;"* and Puritan John Woodbury, who lived at Salem in 1627, wrote, *"they speak in grunts and groans, and while the squaws do all the work, the men seem more interested in lazing about, fishing now and then and drinking uncuppy."* Uncuppy, was what the Indians called whiskey and rum, introduced to them by the White man, and it was a major ingredient in their undoing here in New England. Famous warrior

Red Jacket once told a gathering of Whites, *"We gave your forefathers corn and meat; they gave us poison in return."*

In his 17th century Journal, Jasper Dankaerts, during a visit to Boston, wrote this: *"The people in this place, who are almost all traders in small articles, whenever they see an Indian enter the house who they know has any money, they immediately set about getting hold of him, giving him rum to drink, whereby he is soon caught and becomes half a fool. If he should then buy anything, he is doubly cheated in the wares and in the price. He is then urged to buy more drink, which they now make half water. . . They do not rest until they have cajoled him out of all his money, or most of it. . . Although it is forbidden to sell the drink to the Indians, yet everyone does it."*

Only Roger Williams and his followers who were kicked out of the Puritan settlements to establish the Baptists in Rhode Island, and the Quakers who arrived about 1637, treated the Indians with respect and as equals. Cotton Mather said that the Quakers *"are another sort of enemy, which may with very good reason be cast into the same history with the Indians."* The Quakers constantly harassed the Puritans, interrupting their Sunday meetings and calling them, among other unflattering names, *"Pagan worshippers."* Some Quakers were hanged on Boston Common for their defiance, most were banned from the Bay colony and went to live with Roger Williams in Rhode Island. During King Philip's War, Quakers and Baptists refused to fight the Indians, and although they lived close to many of the battlegrounds, their settlements were never attacked. Increase Mather said of them, *"They set themselves to defend the Indians in their bloody villanies, and revile the country for defending itself against them."* Leading Quaker Thomas Maule retorted, *"God hath well rewarded the inhabitants of New England for their unrighteous dealings towards the native Indians, with a double measure of blood, by fire and sword."*

Of the Puritans it was said, *"Pain is joy and joy is pain."* Their culture was seemingly void of amusements or entertainments, and they loved to punish people. When they tired of expelling and executing Indians and Quakers, they turned to persecuting old women and old men as witches and wizards, a campaign which culminated at Salem in 1692, where over 150 were accused of witchcraft, 19 were hanged, and one eighty-year-old man was crushed to death. Cotton Mather led this fiendish hysteria as well. From his Boston pulpit he announced, *"We deplore witchcraft, and all means must be taken to combat the devil and his works. Witchcraft is a horrible plot against the country, which if not seasonable discovered, will problably blow up and pull down all the churches in the county."*

As Cotton immersed himself in the witch hunt, riding to Salem on a white horse to watch his fellow minister and Harvard Graduate, George Burroughs, hang from a limb at Gallows Hill, his father, the President of Harvard College, was in Plymouth, climbing the pole on which sat the skull of King Philip. He tore off the Chief's jawbone, where birds had been nesting and threw it to the ground, shouting to the crowd of Pilgrims who had gathered to watch him, *"This King Philip was a blasphemous leviathan!"*

Many of America's first settlers came from Essex, England, known for centuries as *"Witch Country,"* by the English, and with them they brought seeds and plants of herbs and drugs to be planted here for foods and medicines. Like the Native Americans, these first New England housewives had to rely on their herb remedies, passed on to them from previous generations, in order that they and their families survive the ills of this new untamed land. Few doctors were willing to begin a new practice in the wilderness, so the early settlers would go to the wise women with herb gardens, or to the Indians, to cure sicknesses. Thus, these women, with their mysterious healing concoctions, were considered witches. It was soon thought that they caused as well as cured illnesses, and when the Puritans needed a new scapegoat, the accusing finger was pointed at them. At least half of those condemned for witchcraft in New England were herb-healers, and most of them were from Essex County, Massachusetts, its shire-town being Salem.

New England's first doctor, and for many years the only one here trained in medicine, was Sam Fuller, who came over on the MAYFLOWER. He constantly complained of overwork and lack of remedies. *"Here, I lose time,"* he wrote, *"and long to be at home. I can do them no good, for I want drugs and things fitting to work with."* Over 50% of the Pilgrims treated by Fuller died in the first year at Plymouth. In 1629 he was called to Salem, where many Puritans who he tried to cure also died, one of them being Governor Endecott's wife. He was also called to the new settlements of Charlestown and Matapan, but was mostly unsuccessful in saving the lives of those suffering from simple fevers and flus. The poor doctor couldn't even save himself, succumbing to a flu virus in 1632.

To fill the void, many ministers dabbled in medicine to save the body as well as the soul, and once again Cotton Mather led the pack as the all-healing Powahee of the White man. His cure for snakebite, which he snitched from the Indians, he sent to the London Royal Society as his own discovery. The leaf of Plantain, he informed them, *"as a poultiss laid to the part bitten, immediately fetches out the deadly poison. It is also remarkable, that if put into the shoes, no serpent will dare to come near them. A tea of it is good Ophtalmiack."* Another self styled doctor, Nicholas Culpepper, suggested the eating of the herb Buglosse as a cure for *"the stings of snakes, spiders and toads.* " In 1651 he wrote, *"This herb also makes a good soup."* " Cotton Mather became so absorbed in what he called, *"the mysteries of medicines"* that he wrote a book on his collected remedies, titled, *"Angel Of Bathesda."* " It was filled with horrible concoctions and *"physicks,"* one being the eating of dried spiders as a cure for hiccups. Mather also initiated the first public inoculation against the most dreaded disease in the Colonies, smallpox. His attempt, however, failed and many died from his inoculations. In posters, broadsides, letters and flyers, Mather was informed by friends and relatives of the victims *"to get back to the pulpit and stay there."*

Doctor Zabdiel Boylston of Boston was the first to inoculate against smallpox, and he was so sure of its success, that his first patient was his own six year old son. But, Bostonians considered a needle in the arm akin to witchcraft, and Doctor Boylston came close to going to the gallows. Smallpox raged in Boston in 1763 for the sixth time in 100 years, and those who didn't die from the disease were disfigured for life with pitted and pock-marked faces. Doctor Joseph Warren, one of the first in the graduating class of Harvard Medical School, successfully inoculated many citizens of the Town, including such notable figures as Paul Revere, John Hancock, and John Adams. A few years later, Doctor Warren was leading the American Revolution. He died bravely at Bunker Hill, after literally giving America its patriotic shot in the arm. He was one of the few doctors of his time who wasn't considered a Quack.

John Winthrop of the Bay Colony, when not engrossed in his gubernatorial duties, found time to write a *"Recipe Book,"* containing many bizarre ingredients for various medicines. He was especially proud of his *"black powder against ye plague, smallpox, purples, all sorts of fevers and poysen; either by way of prevention or after infection."* His magical black powder contained, so the *"Recipe Book"* reveals, *"Toads, as many as you will, alive. Put them into an Earthen Pot, so it be half full, and cover it with an Iron Plate, then overwelme the pot so ye bottom be uppermost; put charcoals round about it and over it and in the open air, not in a house, set it on fire... When it is cold, take out the Toads, and in an iron morter pound them very well and so again. The first time, they will be a brown powder, the next time, black. Of this you may give a dragme or drink inwardly in any infection taken: and let them sweat upon it in their beds: but let them not cover their heads, especially in the small-pox. For prevention half a dragme will suffice."* The Governor warns us, however, that the gathering of the toads should only be in the month of March. Apparently, the toads weren't filled with the right juices during the other months.

Another of Governor Winthrop's favorites was a physic of Rubila, containing nitre and antimony, which smelled so bad that people, especially children, would gag and often throw-up when they had to take it. Winthrop also relied on weird concoctions brewed by a noted Quack alchemist, Sir Kenelm Digby. Digby would ship various mixtures of his own Kickapoo Juice to Massachusetts from England, at Winthrop's request. His healing tonics usually contained: herbs, drugs, roots, seeds, bark, leaves, saps, syrups, powders, plasters, flowers, and of course, alcohol. Each bottle had a kick, and tasted like poo, but the name Kickapoo actually came from a tribe of Indians who excelled at making curative tonics.

The Governor's son John, who became Governor of Connecticut, also considered himself a medicine-man, utilizing many of his father's remedies for various illnesses. Neither Governor made secret the ingredients of their remarkable remedies, and John Jr. was constantly sending letters off to his friends in other parts of New England, listing items that made up potent medicines. Roger Williams, the founder of Rhode Island, was cured of influenza by mail, thanks to the Governor of Connecticut. Governor Endecott and Governor Winthrop of the Bay Colony, were trading medical remedies as early as 1634, and were shipping strange ingredients through the mail as well. *"I have sent you Mrs. Beggarly, her Unicorn's horn and beza stone,"* wrote Endecott to Winthrop, from Salem to Boston. On the return mail, Winthrop sent Endecott: *"mugwort, orgaine and galingall root"*—all mysterious stuff for some wild concoction.

One of their cures was for, believe it or not, *"cheering the heart from grief."* Our first Governors promoted it as a means to *"drive out things ill for the heart, sadness, anger, evil tidings and loss of friends, worms out of the brain, as well as dross out of the stomach,"* The ingredients were as follows: *"Four gallons of strong ale, five ounces of aniseeds, liquorish scraped half a pound, sweet-minta, angelica, eccony, cowslip flowers, sage and Rosemary flowers, sweet marjoram, of each three handfuls, ferment for three days—Juniper berries, bruised one dram, red rosebuds, roasted apples and dates sliced and stoned, of each half a pound, distil again and sweeten with sugarcandy, and take of ambergreese, pearl, red-coral, hartshorn, pounded, of each half a drum, put them in a fine linnen bag and hang them by a thread in a glass."* This *"happy juice"* would obviously take a lot of time and effort to make, and probably just drinking the *"four gallons of strong ale,"* would be enough to *"cheer the heart."*

Zerolabel Endecott, son of the Governor, who embelished some of his father's remedies, had the ultimate solution for a sore throat: *"First bleed and purge with dincassia. After vomiting with vinum-antimonii, rub the tongue with the juice of crabfish and housleck, taking a little inwardly, then. . . the ashes of owl, feathers as well, blown into the throat, opens and breaks the imposthume wonderfully.* '' That same year, 1671, he also revealed his cures for toothaches and deafness. *"For ye toothache, take a little piece of opium,"* he wrote, *"as big as a great pinshead, and put it into the hollow place of the aching tooth, and it will give pleasant ease, often tried by me upon many people and never failed."* And of course, today we know he was absolutely right! I don't think his deafness remedy could have been as successful: *"For deafness or slow hearing,"* his ingredients were: *"the juice of radishes, the fat of mole, an eel and the juice of onion, all soaked in wine and roasted."* Zerolabel doesn't make it quite clear as to whether all this should be eaten, drunk, or dropped into the ear, but he adds as an afterthought, *"boys urine is good,"* which apparently was his secondary cure for deafness.

A popular cure for deafness in the early 1700's was *"Royal Honey-Water,"* which was advertised throughout the colonies as *"an Excellent Perfume, good against Deafness, and to make the hair grow as the directions set forth, is 6d. per bottle and proportionate by the ounce."* Although the ingredients of *"Royal Honey Water"* were never divulged, it too, supposedly contained urine, but its recognizable odor was covered up with *"excellent perfume."*

Strange as it may sound, urine does have restorative qualities, but not for hearing or hair growing. The ancient Europeans and Arabs applied urine to open wounds, often mixed with wine or vinegar, and it was even taken internally as a cure for syphilis. Our American forefathers considered baby urine, swallowed in small doses, as a cure-all for various internal problems, but usually only the urine from male babies was effective. As Zerolabel Endecott points out in his prescription, only *"boys urine is good."*

Many of the medicines prescribed by our first doctors were down right nasty. Doctor Quincy leading physician of the early 18th Century, for example, recommended *"peacock dung"* as a cure for *"epilepsia and vertigo."* He writes in his *"English Dispensatory,"* that *"ashes of the dung of a black cow, given to a new born infant, doth not only preserve from the Epilepsia, but also cures it."* In 1742, Doctor Quincy announced *"goose-dung is reckoned good in distempers of the head,"* and he explains, *"the excrements of most birds are accounted hot, nitrous, and penetrating, for the reason they pass for inciders and detergents."* For palsy, Doctor John Perkins of Boston suggested in 1740, *"take a hot bath in absinthe and urine."* And Doctor Salmon in 1671, recommended the *"fillings of a deadman's skull. . .It is a real cure for falling sickness, vertigo, lethargy, numbness, and all Capital diseases, in which it is a wonderful prevalent.* " To enhance the potency of this sickening cure-all, Doctor Salmon suggests *"diarrhodian, and seeds of peony and miselto,"* be added and made into *"a very fine powder."* He further recommends that the patient *"take of it as will,"* and *"lie it on a skilliney two or three nights together, before the new and the full moon, take with bettony water."* For old people and children who suffer from *"falling-sickness,"* Doctor Salmon decided that the *"fillings of a dead man's skull"* might be too powerful, so he suggests *"the liver of forty water-frogs brought into a powder, and given at five times morning and evening. It will cure those of ripe age,"* he assured the Pilgrims and Puritans, as long as they *"do not eat nor drink two hours before nor after it."* Who could possibly want to eat anything after swallowing the brains of a dead man or the livers of forty frogs!?

One wonders with such nauseating and chilling panaceas, why doctors weren't executed by our forefathers, along with accused witches. Doctor Quincy, who was the most respected of the lot both here and in England, provided at least two remedies that are steeped in superstition and certainly border on witchcraft. For *"sick women,"* he suggests, without mentioning what that sickness might be, *"to take the milk of a nurse that gives suck to a male child and also take a he cat, and cut off one of his ears, or a piece of it, and let it bleed into the milk. Then let the sick woman drink it. Do this three times."* Quincy tries to justify this unorthodox medicine by stating that, *"A creature, whenever it ails anything in the head, it lies in such a posture as to keep one of the tips of a hoof in its ear, which after some time effects a cure."* Apparently Quincy assumed that animals contained a healing potion in their ears. Probably his most diabolical cure was for *"dispersing scrophulous tumours."* He admits that the cure comes from *"some superstitious conceits amongst Common people,"* but that by rubbing the tumor with *"a dead man's hand,"* it will eventually disappear. *"Reports furnish us with many instances of cures done hereby,"* he writes, *"and because the sensation which strooking in that manner gives, is somewhat surprising and occasions a shuddering chillness upon the part touched, which may in many cases put the fibres in such contractions as to loosen, shake off, and dislodge the obstructed matter; in which consists the cure."*

In *"New England Rarities Discovered,"* written by John Josselyn after visits to New England in 1638 and in 1663, he informs England's readers of New Englanders' *"Physical and Chyrurgical Remedies, wherewith the natives constantly use to cure their distempers, wounds, and sores."* He writes that New Englanders rid themselves of toothaches by *"scarifying the gums with a thorn from a dog-fish's back,"* and *"beaver cods are much used for wind in the stomach and belly, particularly of pregnant women."* He seems

Governor John Winthrop—
Massachusetts

Governor John Winthrop
The Younger—Connecticut

Governor John Endecott—
Massachusetts

Reverend Cotton Mather

All self-made doctors and medical Quacks

Photos of portraits courtesy of State House, Boston and Essex Institute, Salem.

obsessed with the trials and tribulations of pregnant women in the New England wilderness, and he offers his own cure for *"sharpe and difficult travel in women with child. . . . Take a lock of Virgins hair on any part of ye head, of half the age of ye woman in travel. Cut it very small to fine powder. Then take twelve ants eggs dried in an oven after ye bread is drawn, or otherwise make them dry and make them to powder with the hair. Give this with a quarter of a pint of red cows milk or for want of it, give it in strong ale wort."* Josselyn also mentions a woman he met who was *"afflicted with a Wolf in her breast,"* a *"Wolf"* being a tumor, which she washed daily *"with rum and arsnick,"* hoping to dissolve the growth. It did work as a cure, but *"her kind husband, who sucked out the poysen as the sore was healing,"* wrote Josselyn, *"lost all his teeth."*

Most of the so-called medicines or cures for a variety of ills, from Colonial days up until the mid-twentieth century, contained generous amounts of alcohol. *"In early times,"* wrote Connecticut historian Samuel Goddrich in 1804, *"rum was largely consumed by the men, and women took their schnapps called 'Hopkins' Elixer,' which was the most delicious and seductive means of getting tipsy that has ever been invented."* The 'Elixer' supposedly provided women with needed iron in their blood, as did Lydia Pinkham's Vegetable Tonic at a later date, which contained eighty percent vegetable juices and twenty percent alcohol. Lydia, a poor girl from Lynn, Massachusetts, became a multi-millionaire selling her tonic and liver pills. I recall as a boy in the early 1940s, *"Lydia Pinkham's Pink Pills,"* were still in demand. Her tonic was a cure-all, advertised as *"the best tonic for female weakness."* Ironically, Lydia was a teatotaler, and a member of the Temperance Society. It wasn't revealed that her miraculous liquid mixture contained alcohol until the late 1900's, and Lydia was well out of the business and the world by then. She had fooled and deceived all of her satisfied clients. Lydia Pinkham is known today as *The Mother of False Advertising*, yet in her day it wasn't required to list ingredients on labels. The only law, passed by Congress in 1848, was *"to prohibit the importation of substitued, adulterated, or substandard drugs,"* and Lydia complied by using the real stuff—there was nothing substandard in her tonic!

From the first landing of Pilgrims and Puritans in New England, beer, ale, wine and strong liquor were used as medicines. Even in ancient Egypt, beer was the cure for scorpion bites, and one Pharaoh left a cryptographic message on his tomb, recently deciphered. It read: *"A delicious remedy against death is half an onion in beer foam."*

The ancient Persians, in attempting to preserve grapes in the off-season, ended up with vats full of rotten grapes. One of them, in an attempt to commit suicide by drinking the vile, rotten liquid the grapes produced, ended up singing, laughing and loving life an hour later. He had discovered wine, still called *"the delisious poison,"* in Persia. A few centuries later in Europe, when University students gathered together to drink beer and wine, they'd *"place a piece of bread parched with heat into their cups,"* to improve the flavor. Today, we leave out the bread, but when gathered with friends, we often clank our glasses together and drink *"toasts."* The word *"whiskey"* came to us from the ancient Celts, as did the drink itself, which in Gaelic means, *"the water of life."* Although it was often mixed in with other ingredients as a cure-all for a variety of ills and diseases, it had been considered since inception as, *"a gift from the Devil."* Some superstitious Colonials believed that demons entered the mouth while drinking whiskey, and only by making a loud verbal cry or grunt before taking a sip of it, could you frighten the demons away. Obviously, after too many sips of whiskey, the demons managed to sneak into the body, and most of us at some time have witnessed the results of mixing demons with whiskey.

Zerolabel Endecott, concocted many alcohol remedies in the 1600's. His *"recipe"* for stones in the bladder or kidneys, *"or to prevent it,"* was to *"take wild carrot seeds and boil them in ale, then drink a dose three times every night."* His brew for ridding oneself of witches, or a witches curse, was made up of: *"castor oil, coral jasper, menstrual blood, sweet-flag, resin and fragrant sandal, all mixed into 3½ quarts of brandy."* Even after drinking only one quart of this stuff, a witch wouldn't come near you. Zerolabel's cure for measles, which was a serious disease in those days, was *"a pinch of soot and a raw egg in a glass of white wine."* For the common cold, the good doctor recommended, *"a glass of hot wine with nine drops of beeswax, to be taken before bed."*

A Doctor Ball of Northboro, Massachusetts had a powerful mixture he prescribed for a condition he called, *"the scratches."* It was obviously some kind of skin-itch, possibly poison-ivy, hives, or rickets. But he doesn't reveal whether his mixture should be rubbed on the itchy skin or swallowed. *"Take one quart of fishworms, washed clean, and stew together with one pound of hog's lard,"* writes Doctor Ball. *"Filter it all through a strainer, adding one half-pint of turpentine and one half-pint of good brandy."* In a postscript he adds, *"simmer it well and it is fit for use."* He probably meant for the mixture to be consumed, but I wouldn't want to be the first to taste it, itch or no itch. Doctor Quincy of the English Dispensatory, whose cures for every conceivable ailment usually contained alcohol, were prescribed constantly here in New England. He relied heavily on alcohol because it not only killed germs and made the patients feel good, but it disguised the true identity of some of his other ingredients. It also conceivably killed a few patients!

One of Quincy's own inventions was *"Hog-lice Wine."* It was an *"admirable medicine against jaundice, dropsy, or any cachectic habits,"* wrote Doctor Quincy. The ingredients were: *"Half a pound of wood lice or sowbugs, put them alive into two pounds of white port wine, and after some days infusion, strain and press out very hard. Then, put in saffron, two drams, salt of steel, a dram, and salt of amber, two scruples, and after three or four days, strain and filter for use."* I don't know what dropsy or cachectic habits are, but I once suffered from jaundice and was told that the one drink to never consume was wine. My doctor told me that it was even dangerous to drink wine months after the jaundice had subsided, so Doctor Quincy probably lost a lot of his patients with his Hog-lice Wine. Doctor Quincy also came out with another strange cure for jaundice in 1742. He said, *"Let the sick person drink their own urine twice a day, morning and evening in Posset Ale."*

"Crying babies were silenced with hot toddy," wrote Samuel Goddrich, *"then esteemed an infallible remedy for Wind in the Stomach."* Colonial babies often suffered from worms and rickets, and the most prescribed medicine for these ailments was snail-water mixed with various forms of alcohol. The home remedy was to *"gather a peck of garden snails, wash them off with beer, wipe them of the green froth, and bruise the shells in a stone morter. Then slit open a quart of earthworms, scour with salt and beat them in the stone morter to little pieces. Add angelica, celandine, rosemary flowers, bearsfoot, agrimony, red dock roots, bark of barberries, betony wood sorel, of each two handfulls, and one handful of rue. Pour on three gallons of strong ale and set it to stand all night. Take the water of it, two spoonfuls, and four spoonfulls of small beer—that is the cure for rickets."* In the 1700's, you could buy similar ingredients all mixed into a bottle, called *"Daffy's Elixer,"* which was advertised in the Boston papers as the cure for an infant's *"fits, worms, and rickets."*

"Daffy's Elixer," which was very popular, probably killed a lot of kids and may be where we get the expression, *"He's gone a little daffy."* In fact, it seems that many Colonial doctors with their disgusting and often dangerous remedies, were a bit daffy, but there were few if any medical schools in those days, hardly any medical books, and no hospitals. The only way a person could learn about medicine and healing was to serve an old doctor for a number of years, and hope that the old doctor wasn't a quack. To the first wave of settlers, witches with their herb gardens, and Indian medicine men with their spiritual rituals, often brought better results in healing than did the local doctors.

Many families in the 17th and early 18th centuries set aside a plot near the home for a herb garden. The three most popular plants in the garden being *"caraway, dill and fennel,"* known in early days as the *"meeting seeds."* People would be constantly munching on them at religious services to keep them awake during boring sermons. Caraway, like Mather's powdered spiders, was thought to stop hiccuping; and dill would prevent rickets. It was fennel that really did help keep the chewing parishioners awake. Cotton Mather, like Josselyn, listed what he considered the most useful medicinal plants in early New England. They were: *"alehoof, garlic, elder, sage, rue and saffron."* Samuel Goodrich writes that he remembered vividly as a boy seeing *"a labyrinth displayed in the garret,"* today called the attic, *"of dried fruits, amid bunches of summer savory, boneset, fennel and other herbs, hung in festoons upon the rafters."* He also recalled that, *"the juice of the ash tree was the sovereign antidote for the ear-ache."* Actually, the seeds, roots, stems, flowers and juices, of almost every weed, plant and tree found in New England, were utilized by the Indians and Colonials for food, perfumes, dyes, charms, or medicines. Every plant growing wild here was considered a weed until some use was found for it. As Ralph Waldo Emerson said, *"A weed is a plant whose virtues have not yet been discovered."*

Many of the so-called weeds of New England were utilized to cure common ailments in olden days, and to a certain extent, are still being utilized today: Snakeroot for fevers, daisy-roots for earaches, chamomile for stomachaches, dandelion juice for liver problems, tansy for bruises, plantain for insect bites, anise seeds for insomnia; rue helps breathing, savory helps digestion, wood bettony for cramps, yarrow for wounds, penyroyal stays vomiting. The list, although not unending, extends into the hundreds of weeds, herbs and flowers that are still used for medicinal purposes. The healing qualities of some go back to ancient times. The mustard seed was considered an antidote in Biblical times, and Roman historian Pliny wrote, *"It revives hysterical women."* It is still used for colds, gout, poor circulation and rhuematism, and, of course, remains a staple spice on the dinner table.

Since ancient times, when Druids, soothsayers and witches consulted dead chickens to predict the future (by searching through the entrails), many foods were considered either good or bad for consumption. Onions were eaten as a physic, and when held to a sore or diseased eye, would heal it. *"Onions applyed to a wound, cure the bitings of mad dogs,"* wrote Nicholas Culpepper in 1653, *"and when roasted and applyed to boils, it helps,"* he said. To cure the deadly disease of scurvy, ancient mariners drank a tea made from the needles of the hemlock tree, English tars sucked on limes, thus their nickname *"Limeys."* And New England sailors munched on Cape Code cranberries, none or them realizing that scurvy is caused by a lack of vitamin

C in the system. Lettuce *"cools inflamations of the stomach and resists drunkeness,"* says Culpepper, and carrots *"improves ones sight."* For colds, *"castor and oil, sulfer and molasses,"* or *"cod livers,"* would prevent them or cure them. I still cringe at the large spoonfuls of cod-liver oil I was forced to take as a child every early spring and autumn. Fig juice is an ancient remedy for sickness of the stomach and bowels. And its cousin prune juice is still the best remedy for constipation, especially when you consider Doctor Quincy's solution for the same internal problems was *"donkey dung and flyspecks."*

"An apple a day keeps the doctor away," was a popular saying when I was a boy, and many mothers followed the saying religiously, making sure their offspring consumed that apple. I constantly prodded my mother that the same apple could be put into a pie and be just as healthful. Apples, like the *"sacred cod,"* were precious to Colonial New Englanders, and in 1733, Reverend Samuel Deane of Maine wrote a controversial article for *"The New England Farmer,"* concerning the harvesting of apples. *"Gather apples at noon on the day of the full moon,"* the minister insisted, *"for as we know, both animals and vegetables are influenced by the moon in some cases, why may we not suppose a greater quantity of spirit is sent up into the fruit, when the attraction of the heavenly bodies is greatest?"* Some farmers thought it sacrilege that a minister followed the signs of the moon, much like the witches did. But most were just angry that he not only told them how they should live each Sunday, but was now preaching to them how they should do their job. Ministers, it seems, throughout America's early history, even after Cotton Mather was forced to *"stay in the pulpit,"* continued in their attempts to be farmers, teachers and doctors.

The inscription on the gravestone of a prominent Puritan minister at Malden, Massachusetts, reads: *"Reverend Michael Wigglesworth, died 1705—Here lies intered in silent grave below, Malden's Physician for soul and body too."* Wigglesworth prescribed *"a salve of honey and cornmeal applied to the eye for pig-sties, and pour red pepper in your stockings and in your tea for chills."* He also suggested *"saltpork applied to heal wounds,"* and many of his other remedies included foodstuffs that the housewife would have readily available when someone was in need of nursing.

Another man-of-the-cloth who dabbled in medicine and often doubled as a doctor, was Reverend Thomas Smith of the first church in Portland, Maine. He began *"his ardous duties"* writes his biographer, William Willis, *"in 1727, being extended over a large territory. . . . Nor were his labors confined to pastoral duties. He was,"* writes Willis, *"equally devoted to those of the medical profession, and references to this medical practice are numer-*

ous in his Journal. . . His ministrations were as eagerly sought for bodily relief as for solace and instructions of religion. . . . His wit and humor were fresh and free, and at times hardly restrained within clerical lines. "He was in Portland, then known as Falmouth, when British ships bombarded and destroyed the town in 1775, his house being the last to burn to the ground. With tears in his eyes, he treated the many burn victims with his famous wet-tea leaves solution applied to the burnt skin. Tea was the most common drink in New England prior to the Revolution, but few drank tea during and after the war. It was often used for medicinal purposes, especially for colds and bronchitis. Cornsilk tea was consumed for kidney problems and ginseng and spikeroot tea for tonsilitis. Reverend Smith often used tea leaves moistened and applied to cuts, burns and skin itches. Another Colonial cure for burns was mashed potatoes and butter. Smith also used puffball mushrooms to stop bleeding, and gilead buds (cloves) and alcohol for cuts and bruises.

"Reverend McGee's wife died from eating thirteen chickens and drinking strong beer and flip," said Dr. John Perkins of Boston, in 1742, *"only thirteen days after giving birth."* Perkins considered himself an expert on foods that would hurt and foods that would heal. He hated alcohol in any form as a drink, but often prescribed it as a medicine, even to children. *"Castile soap boiled in warm beer,"* was his cure for stomach trouble. *"Whiskey, honey and butter,"* he recommended for bronchitis, and *"turnip-root for fevers—eat it,"* he said. *"Boiled vinegar for a cold,"* and *"warm milk and molasses for coughs."* All but the soap in beer sound like perfectly legitimate cures, but it seems that once Doctor Perkins detracts from food as medicine, he enters the medical world of quackery. For example, he wrote, *"For weak eyes, you should shave your head."* His counterpart, Dr. Benjamin Bullivant, was held in high regard for prescribing various combinations of spices, herbs and foods for healing and for better health. His biographer said, *"to the poor he always prescribed cheap, but wholesome medicines. . . . not directing them to the East Indies to look for drugs, when they may have for better out of their gardens."* Doctor Bullivant recommended *"rhubarb for inward bruises, red pepper paste for shingles,"* and *"chammomile and brown bread crumbs for insomnia."* Doctor Perkins disagrees with Doctor Bullivant on his insomnia cure. *"Justice Billings died from eating brown bread,"* said Perkins. *"For insomnia,"* Perkins recommended, *"applying a hard boiled egg to the nape of the neck, peeled."*

Some superstitious New Englanders actually wore certain items of food around their neck or wrist, believing it would prevent certain illnesses or diseases, or to cure them of some sickness they already had. It was believed that nutmeg worn on a string or necklace would prevent lice or boils, and that saltpork similiarly worn would ward off chills and colds. A corn-kernel necklace would prevent or cure headaches; and a ring of dried raw potato peels worn on the middle finger of either hand, would ease the pain of arthritis—much like people wear copper bracelets for the same effect today. It was thought that a horse-chestnut carried in the pocket would also help cure arthritis. Puritan boys and girls wore tansey bags around their necks and pressed to the chest all winter long to defend themselves from rheumatism. The Puritan adults ate the tansey root as a remedy for gout, and tansey was used for cooking.

"*I do not consider myself as hazarding anything,*" wrote Queen Anne's physician, Doctor Lister in 1656, "*when I say no man can be a good physician who has not a competent knowledge of cooking.*" Some of New England's doctors were cooks, and a few wrote cookbooks, and still others attempted to blend their so-called skills by publishing healing recipes in the newspapers. The **Boston Evening Post** in 1771 provided a series on the proper ingredients to solve the sufferings of sick children: "*Senna and Rhubarb and Snails, with a mixture of prunes, to be used for Collick and Stomack aches,*" was one solution, "*and to make the childrens first teeth come out without paine.*" The Post reporter gave this recipe: "*Take the head of a Hare, boiled and mingle honey with the brain, and butter, and therewith anoynt the childrens gums. Also, scratch the child's gums with an osprey bone, or hang fawn's teeth or wolfs' fangs around his neck.*"

If one didn't realize how seriously the doctors and patients cherished these healing recipes, it would be a laughing matter. One complicated conglomeration called, "*The Water Of Life,*" which was sold as a cure-all health tonic, emphasizes why a doctor had to have a competent knowledge of cooking. The recipe for "*The Water of Life,*" was kept secret by doctors during much of the 17th century, but when the ingredients were revealed, it was obvious that whoever conceived it was a madman:
"*Balm leaves and stalks and flowers, Rosemary, red sage, Targon, Torment Leaves, Rossolis and roses, Carnation Hyssop, Thyme, red strings that grow upon Savory, red Fennel leaves and root, red mints, of each a handful; bruise these herbs and put them in a great earthen pot and pour on them enough white wine as will cover them, and let them steep for nine days. Then put in Cinnemon, Ginger, Angelica seeds, Cloves and Nutmeg, of each one ounce, a little Saffron, Sugar one pound, Raysins solis stoned, one pound, and loyns and legs of an old coney, a fleshy running capon, the red flesh of the sinews of a leg of mutton, four young chickens, twelve larks and yokes of twelve eggs, a loaf of white bread, cut in sops, and three ounces of Mithridate, and as much Muscadine as will cover them all. Distil all with a moderate fire, and keep the waters by themselves, and when there comes no more by distilling, put more wine into the pot upon the same stuff and distil it again,*"

and you shall have another good water.''

How could our forefathers persecute so-called witches for concocting their weird brews, when the doctors themselves were feeding a mess like this to the public? It was supposedly the health-tonic of the times and was advertised to *"Strengthen the Spirit, Brain, Heart, Liver and Stomack. Take when need is by itself, or with Ale, Beer or Wine mingled with Sugar."* This is what the old-timers called Kickapoo Juice, and they thrived on it. Those who couldn't stomach the smell and taste of it, would rub it on their bodies—it had the same effect.

Whenever I open a jar of pickles, I think of my departed father. The smell of vinegar always reminds me of him, for he not only drank glasses of it regularly, but he rubbed his chest and legs with it almost every other day. Vinegar was his miraculous cure-all, but he died of cancer from smoking, just after his seventieth birthday, still smelling of vinegar. Many of these *"Chyrugeons, Quacksalvers,"* and *"Charlatans,"* as they came to be called, sold salves, unguents and tonics door to door, town to town, shouting the praises of their marvelous mixtures. By the mid 18th century, the names *Kickapoo Juice, Snakeoil and Skunkoil''* were the popular names given to all such medicinal tonics. The ingredients of all of them were usually kept secret by the creators, so that one quack doctor wouldn't steal the recipe from another. One secret curing tonic that could be taken internally or externally, its contents revealed only after its service to the sick was no longer required, consisted of: *"Three ounces of fine seed pearls in distilled vinegar, and when perfectly dissolved, drop a few drops of oil tarter upon it, and it will call down the pearl into powder, then put to it spring water."* My father would have loved it!

Besides pearls, gold, ivory, rubies, and coral were often used in medicines after being pulverized into powders. Ivory was sometimes passed on as being *"Unicorn horns,"* and was often called *"Alehood."* Peppermint and spearmint were often added for taste; and various perfumes, to hide the foul odors of some of the ingredients. One of Doctor Quincy's favorites was *"Herring in pickle,"* which he suggested be *"used in a cataplasm to the feet to dispel fevers, because it is recond to draw humours downward and thereby relieve the head."* Lady Spencer, a noted candy maker of Salem in the 18th century, had her own sweet cure for gout and smallpox, *"green turf of grass, but use the green side not the dirt side,"* she suggested. Quincy did her one better, when he recommended *"the moss that groweth in a well, mixed with cat's blood, and so apply it warm to the place where the shingles be."* For an eye-salve, Sir Edward Spencer, Lady Spencer's son, prescribed *"crushed pearls and ten skins of adder snakes, mixed into a powder."* Another Salemite, noted sea captain Sam Ingersoll, announced his formula in 1685 for making hair grow. *"Take some fire-flies and some red worms,"* he said, *"and black snails and some humbees, dry them and pound them to a mix in milk or water."* He had to be kidding! However, then as now, there were many hairgrowing remedies readily purchased by anxious bald headed men and women. One such ointment consisted of, *"dry leaves of sunflowers mixed with vegtable oil, rub into the scalp once a day for eight weeks;"* and another was made up of *"honey and pulverated vine twigs."*

There were, of course, many old fashioned remedies that worked well, and some are still being used today, but not necessarily as medicines. American Indians assured the first Whites that landed here that the bark of the Cinchona Tree, when chewed, dispelled fevers. We consume it today as *"quinine,"* the treatment for malaria, and it also goes well with gin. Doctor James Salisbury recommended ground up beef as a cure for rheumatism and gout in 1888, and thus presented England with *"Salisbury Steaks,"* and America with *"Hamburgers."* A thick brown aphrodisiac liquid, thought to cure dysentery, and used as a divine stimulant by South American Indians, we know it today as *Chocolate*. Another stimulating panacea, thought by old New Englanders to cure smallpox, is now America's favorite drink—*Coffee*.

With all the trial and error experienced by the Indians and America's first settlers, it's a wonder any of our ancestors survived. But, we haven't found perfection yet. There are still charlatans out there, ready to sell us miraculous remedies for whatever ails us. Although we like to think differently, we are still often motivated by the customs of our parents and grandparents, or the suggestions of friends, to take this or that recommended cure-all for some specific ailment or injury. Few of us are even aware of the chemicals we consume, sometimes on a daily basis, to motivate or stimulate ourselves, or to just make ourselves feel better.

Some 400 years from now a little book will be written to titillate our descendents. It will tell of our taking a thick milky substance that tasted like chalk to relieve constipation, or little chocolate bars to accomplish the same thing. Hundreds of companies manufactured this little white pill, sometimes coating it with different colors, as a cure-all for many ills, but it was just the same product with many names, which was called aspirin. And they actually sprayed all their vegetable gardens and fruit orchards with poisons, apparently to kill weeds and bugs, but then they ate the vegetables and fruit, and in the process, poisoned themselves. It must have been a strange world then, when people were dying from heart-attacks and a thing called cancer. How misguided they were.

The only statue in New England dedicated to the Kickapoo Juice sales-man and medicine-man—always with an empty bottle of medicine or whiskey clutched in his hand—is actually famous 19th century aboli-tionist, William Lloyd Garrison, located in downtown Newburyport, Massachusetts.

Olde New England's Curious Customs & Cures
Bibliography

Benedict, William, *History Of Sutton, Massachusetts,* with Rev. Hiram Tracy—1878.

Bliss, William Root, *The Old Colony Town And Other Sketches,* Houghton Mifflin Company, Boston, MA—1893.

Bonfanti, Leo, *Biographies and Legends of New England Indians,* Volumes I - V, Pride Publications, Wakefield, MA—1976.

Botkin, B.A., *A Treasury of New England Folklore,* American Legacy Press (1901), Bonanza Books, New York, N.Y.—1965.

Brasch, R., *How Did It Begin,* David McKay Company, New York—1966.

Browne, Waldo G., *Real Legends of New England,* Albert Whitman And Company, Chicago, Ill.—1930.

Calverton, V.F., *The Awakening of America,* The John Day Company, New York, N.Y.—1939.

Carper, Jean, *The Food Pharmacy,* Bantam Books, New York—1988.

Densmore, Francis, *How Indians Use Wild Plants For Food, Medicine And Crafts,* Dover Publications, New York—1928.

Drake, Samuel Adams, *A Book Of New England Legends And Folklore,* Charles E. Tuttle Company, Rutland, Vt.—1884-1971.

Drimmer, Frederick, *Captured By The Indians,* Dover Publications, New York—1961.

Earle, Alice Morse, *Customs And Fashions In Old New England,* Charles Scribner's Sons, New York—1893. Charles E. Tuttle Co., Rutland, Vt.—1973.

Griffis, William Elliot, *The Romance Of American Colonization,* W.A. Wilde and Company, Boston, MA—1898.

Jilek, Doctor Wolfgang G., *Indian Healing,* Hancock House Publishers, Blaine, Washington—1982.

Kamm, Minnie Watson, *Old Time Herbs For Northern Gardens,* Little, Brown And Company, New York—1938.

Stark, Raymond, *Guide To Indian Herbs,* Hancock House Publishers, Blaine, Washington—1981.

Stimpson, George, *A Book About American History,* Harper And Brothers Publishers, New York—1950.

Travers, Milton A., *The Wampanoag Indian Federation,* The Christopher Publishing House, Boston, MA—1957.

Verrill, Hyatt, *American Indian,* D. Appleton And Company, New York—1927.